Publications of the

MINNESOTA HISTORICAL SOCIETY

RUSSELL W. FRIDLEY
Editor and Director

JUNE DRENNING HOLMQUIST
Associate Editor

Abraham Lincoln
and His Mailbag

TWO DOCUMENTS BY EDWARD D. NEILL,

ONE OF LINCOLN'S SECRETARIES

Edited by THEODORE C. BLEGEN

Minnesota Historical Society   St. Paul   *1964*

COPYRIGHT, 1964 © BY THE MINNESOTA HISTORICAL SOCIETY, ST. PAUL
Library of Congress Catalog Card Number: 64-23313

The author of this publication was aided by a research grant from the Louis W. and Maud Hill Family Foundation to the Minnesota Historical Society.

Contents

Introduction. By THEODORE C. BLEGEN   1

Reminiscences of the Last Years of President Lincoln's Life. By EDWARD D. NEILL   24

President Lincoln's Mail Bag. By EDWARD D. NEILL   46

Introduction

THE RECENT ASSASSINATION of another American President lends poignancy to Edward Duffield Neill's recollections of Abraham Lincoln and his mailbag as presented in the two documents here printed. Apart from that interest, however, the reminiscences of Neill — recorded two decades after the close of the Civil War — are of value as firsthand accounts of events, viewed from the central spot in the nation, in a crowded year of American history. They also constitute an informed appraisal of Lincoln by an observer from within the White House who worked as a member of the President's secretarial staff. Neill was on duty there more than a year, up to the tragic scenes of April 14 and 15, 1865 — and thereafter he continued in service under President Andrew Johnson.

Neill read the first of these papers, entitled *Reminiscences of the Last Year of President Lincoln's Life,* on November 4, 1885, at a meeting in St. Paul of the Minnesota Commandery of the Military Order of the Loyal Legion, a society represented by many branches in the northern states and made up of officers who had served in the federal forces in the Civil War. The address was printed in the same year by the Pioneer Press Company of St. Paul as a paper-bound pamphlet of eighteen pages, copies of which are now relatively rare. It was reprinted in a volume of articles by sundry authors published at St. Paul in 1887 by the Minnesota Commandery of the Loyal Legion. The volume, first in a series of six (the second and third edited by Neill), bore the title *Glimpses of the Nation's Struggle*.[1]

Neill's account has been used by some, but not many, historians, notably by Carl Sandburg; and in 1945 its text was reprinted with a brief foreword in a book of selected articles edited by Rufus R. Wilson and issued in a limited edition.[2] One may safely conclude that, although Neill's narrative is known to some Lincoln scholars, it is little known to the public.

Less known, if not unknown, is the second paper by Neill. Like the first, it was based on his experiences in the Executive Mansion (as the White House was usually called in Lincoln's time). This was his description of "President Lincoln's Mail Bag." In the Neill Papers of the Minnesota Historical Society, this paper survives in two versions. One is the original manuscript, in Neill's handwriting, and another is a typewritten copy with a prefatory note which makes it clear that the copy was made long after Neill's death.[3]

No evidence has been found that Neill ever published this paper, but his manuscript bears the crossed-out inscription "For Cross and Crown," plus the words "Number One." We thus have a clue to the origin and date of the essay. In 1872 Neill started publication of a monthly paper entitled *Cross and Crown*, "devoted to . . . higher education" and especially to Jesus College, a school in

[1] The text of the address as reprinted here is taken from *Glimpses of the Nation's Struggle*, 1:29–53 (St. Paul, 1887). It seems likely that this version was edited by Neill himself. For some reason he omitted one paragraph that appeared in the pamphlet and this has been restored by the present editor. A note will indicate where the paragraph has been inserted. Copies of both works are in the Minnesota Historical Society's library.

[2] Sandburg, *Abraham Lincoln: The War Years*, 3:534; 4:37, 250, 267 (New York, 1939); Wilson, *Intimate Memories of Lincoln*, 599–614 (Elmira, N.Y., 1955). It is of interest to note that Mr. Wilson closes his very brief introductory comments about Neill with the words: "And than he no man more clearly measured the greatness of Abraham Lincoln" (p. 599).

[3] After the death of Neill in 1893, his papers were given to the Society by his daughter, Miss Minnesota Neill, in four installments, in 1909, 1915, 1928, and 1930.

St. Anthony, Minnesota, that he was then promoting in conjunction with the Baldwin Grammar School, a preparatory institution. *Cross and Crown* appeared only as volume 1, number 1, for July, 1872, and the mailbag essay was not included. It seems probable that Neill intended to write a series of articles for this little magazine and therefore marked the essay "Number One." It seems equally probable that he wrote the paper in 1872. It is curious that he did not publish it in some form then or later (as far as is known), for he almost never held anything back from publication save his letters and rough notes. Indeed, the wonder is that he did not write a book about his experiences as a Presidential secretary. It may be noted that he signed the paper with the pseudonym "Scriba" — one of several pseudonyms, including "Rambler" and "Dellian," that he liked to use.[4] Just when the typed copy in the possession of the Minnesota Historical Society was made is not known, though it could not have been until after 1909, when the Society received the first installment of the Neill Papers, and it may have been after 1915. The fact that at some time the copy was typed makes it seem probable that the mailbag piece was printed somewhere, but no reference to its publication has been found.[5]

[4] Neill's pseudonyms may be found among the many clippings that he kept of his newspaper writings. They are preserved in notebooks in the Neill Papers. The Minnesota Historical Society has a copy of the single number of *Cross and Crown*.

[5] The mailbag article is not listed in Richard Booker, *Abraham Lincoln in Periodical Literature 1860–1940* (Chicago, 1941); nor is there any reference to it as a separate publication in James Monaghan's *Lincoln Bibliography, 1839–1939* (2 vols., Springfield, Ill., 1943–45). The absence of the title in these publications, however, does not preclude the possibility that the essay appeared somewhere in a newspaper or magazine. In any event, some scholars have known of its existence. An article on "The Executive Mansion Secretariat," in *Lincoln Lore*, no. 1061, August 8, 1949 (Fort Wayne, Indiana), gives some information about Neill and adds, "Neill prepared a manuscript entitled 'President Lincoln's Mail Bag' which was supposed to have been deposited with the Minnesota Historical Society, but correspondence in 1941 failed to locate this valuable essay." The Society's file of correspondence discloses a letter written on April 29, 1941, by Louis A. Warren, the editor of *Lincoln Lore*, in which he refers to an undated newspaper clipping about a manuscript

One cannot appraise these writings about Lincoln without knowing something of Neill and his background.[6] He was born in Philadelphia on August 9, 1823, the son of a well-known physician of that city and the grandson, on his mother's side, of one of the founders of the College of Physicians of Philadelphia. Two of his brothers, John and Thomas, also had noteworthy careers. During the Civil War, John established the first United States Military Hospital in Philadelphia; and Thomas, a graduate of the United States Military Academy, was an officer who fought at Chancellorsville and Gettysburg, was brevetted brigadier general in the regular army in 1865, and served as commandant at West Point from 1875 to 1879.[7]

Edward, when he was about nineteen, was graduated from Amherst College — he had spent two preparatory years at the University of Pennsylvania and three at Amherst. He then studied for a year at the Andover Theological Seminary, after which he completed his preparation for the ministry in Philadelphia, tutoring with a local pastor. He soon felt himself drawn to the West as a field of service, and in 1847 he was licensed to preach and began his ministry among the lead miners in the vicinity of Galena, Illinois. He was ordained in

in the Society's possession. This clipping, wrote Mr. Warren, said that "Mr Neill had much first hand evidence on Lincoln's correspondence." He made no allusion to the title "President Lincoln's Mail Bag." The Society's curator of manuscripts, Dr. Grace Lee Nute, replied on May 6, 1941, that she had not located any "single manuscript of the kind that you seem to have had in mind when you wrote."

[6] The chief biographical sources for the life of Neill, apart from his own printed and manuscript records, are Huntley Dupre, *Edward Duffield Neill: Pioneer Educator* (St. Paul, 1949); Solon J. Buck's article on Neill in *Dictionary of American Biography*, 13:408 (New York, 1934); a series of well-written essays on Neill in *The Mac 1930* (the yearbook of Macalester College, St. Paul); an account (by Neill himself) in *Historical Notes on the Ancestry and Descendants of Henry Neill, M.D.* (privately printed, St. Paul[?], 1886); and an appreciative essay on "Edward D. Neill, Apostle of Education," in William W. Folwell, *History of Minnesota*, 4:434–442 (St. Paul, 1930).

[7] The three Neill brothers are dealt with, one after the other, in *Dictionary of American Biography*, 13:408–410.

INTRODUCTION 5

1848, and in 1849 he went to St. Paul, the capital of the newly formed Territory of Minnesota. There he began his work as an emissary of the American Home Missionary Society.[8]

This move to Minnesota in its pioneering days launched Neill on a career in which his native versatility had exuberant play. In not a few respects he reminds one of the men of the eighteenth-century Enlightenment whose interests had few boundaries. Neill was a preacher, organizer of churches, lecturer, historian, educator, army chaplain, Presidential secretary, consular official, founder of a college, and a professor. Above all, he was a writer, publicist, and an avid promoter of causes, institutions, and ideas.

In St. Paul he quickly established a meeting place and led in the organization of the First Presbyterian Church, of which he was the minister from 1849 to 1854. By the mid-fifties he had founded yet another church of that denomination, the House of Hope, and he was its minister from 1855 to 1860. He was very active as a lecturer, but he had not been long in Minnesota before his more basic interest in scholarship and writing, particularly in history, found rich outlet. In his historical work he proved himself resourceful in gathering up materials from far and near and in seizing upon subjects close to his environment. In Minnesota he turned to the history of that frontier community in its range from Indian and French times to the mid-nineteenth century; and later, when his career took him East, he explored sources for American colonial history, especially of Maryland and Virginia.

Neill was a charter member of the Minnesota Historical Society, founded in 1849. At its first annual meet-

[8] The Minnesota Historical Society has some of Neill's early Minnesota letters in the American Home Missionary Society Papers, a collection of microfilmed and typewritten copies of letters sent by missionaries in Minnesota to the home office in New York. The originals of the letters, which cover the period from 1849 to 1893, are in the library of the Chicago Theological Society.

ing, held on January 1, 1850, he delivered an address on the French voyageurs in Minnesota, based on original materials.[9] To the pioneers he gave a piece of cogent advice. " 'Write your history as you go along,' " he said, "and you will confer a favor upon the future inhabitants of Minnesota, for which they will be ever grateful." In 1851 he was chosen as the secretary of the Society — its administrative officer — and he served in that capacity officially until 1863, though actually he left the state for the Civil War in 1861.

Neill's most noteworthy contribution to western American history was a monumental one-volume *History of Minnesota* which, almost incredibly, he completed and published by 1858, the year in which Minnesota became the thirty-second state of the Union. This book came out in several editions, enlarged and improved — its fifth edition in 1883 consisted of 929 pages. The work is so rich in its use of documentary sources, so solid and generally objective, that even today, more than a century after it was written, it commands scholarly respect. Of this book, as of his later volumes of colonial history, it may fairly be said that he proved himself a diligent searcher for records, critical in their use, but not especially adept in the organization of his materials. His work was done before the day of training in seminars of history, but in many respects it evidenced professional character. His own conception of what he called "the essential of the historian" he summed up thus: "neither to state false things nor suppress the truth" (*nec falsa dicere, nec vera reticere*). Coupled with his zeal for scholarship was a veritable passion for breaking into print. His love of publication was demonstrated again and again through many years. An evidence of it was the issuance in 1858 of a special, highly illustrated edition

---

[9] Neill's address, "The French Voyageurs to Minnesota during the Seventeenth Century," was published in the Society's *Annals* for 1850 and is included in the *Minnesota Historical Collections*, 1:1-18 (reprint edition, 1902). It is one of many articles by Neill in the early volumes of the Society's *Collections*.

of his *History of Minnesota,* limited to one hundred copies.¹⁰

Neill's contributions to history were only a part of the many-pronged activities that stirred his curiosity and engaged his efforts. He had a lifelong interest in schools, in their full range from the elementary level to college and university, including private academies in the era antedating public high schools. Neill had a promoter's zeal, and he translated interest into action. Soon after his arrival in Minnesota he lent his efforts to the starting of public schools in St. Paul, and in 1851 he moved onto a wider stage as territorial superintendent of schools. He was an outspoken defender of the public schools and made no secret of his opposition to those who attacked the system on religious grounds. He emphasized the nurture of citizenship by the public schools, with special reference to the education of the children of many nationalities crowding into the West. He called for "better school houses," attractive school surroundings, good textbooks, and public recognition of the dignity of the profession of teaching.

At the same time Neill was actively interested in private academies, and one result of this interest was the Baldwin School, launched in St. Paul in 1853, with financial encouragement from Mathias W. Baldwin, the head of the Baldwin Locomotive Works in Philadelphia. This was originally intended as a school for girls, but it admitted young boys as well. The enterprise had scarcely been initiated when Neill started another institution. This was the College of St. Paul, which he believed would help to meet, in a youthful country, the demand "for practical men rather than complete scholars." His plan for studies included civil engineering, chemistry,

¹⁰ The full title of Neill's book, which was published in Philadelphia, was *The History of Minnesota: From the Earliest French Explorations to the Present Time,* and the first edition contained 628 pages; subsequent ones were dated 1873, 1878, 1882, and 1883. Copies of all the editions, including the limited one of 1858, are in the library of the Minnesota Historical Society.

geology, and mechanics, but he did not omit the history of the United States. Baldwin also helped him get this institution started, but debts soon accumulated and the school was poverty-stricken. With masterly understatement Neill explained that the college had been "impeded by the financial revulsion of 1857." If, as Solon J. Buck has suggested, these pioneer institutions were abortive, they nevertheless were prologue to a successful private college in the post-Civil War era.[11]

Meanwhile, in the 1850s Neill's school interests found yet other channels of expression. From 1856 to 1859 he served on the Board of Education in St. Paul and as *ex officio* superintendent of schools. In 1858 he was chosen chancellor of the University of Minnesota, which he had helped to found in 1851 and which was in sad need of reorganization. He helped to devise a reorganization bill that became law in 1860, and he was then again elected chancellor.[12] From this largely nominal post he resigned in 1861, but was prevailed upon to withdraw his resignation, and the office had some kind of dim existence until 1864, though Neill himself, as has been noted, left Minnesota in 1861. Even these events did not quite complete the story of Neill's early educational adventures, for on March 7, 1861, the legislature named him state superintendent of public instruction. (Actually in 1860 as the university chancellor he was state superintendent *ex officio*.) The office was one of very short duration for him, however, because of the Civil War.

The educational history of Dr. Neill cannot be traced in its full extent in this introduction, but it should be noted that the Minnesota historian, William W. Folwell, characterizes Neill as the state's "Apostle of Education"

[11] Dupre, *Neill*, 59, 61; Buck, in *Dictionary of American Biography*, 13:408. The private college was Macalester College, officially opened in 1885.

[12] For Neill's connection with the infant University of Minnesota, see James Gray, *The University of Minnesota 1851–1951*, 23 (Minneapolis, 1951), and Blegen, "A State University Is Born," in *The Land Lies Open*, 151–195 (Minneapolis, 1949).

and Buck, after reviewing Neill's career, speaks of him as a "prophet of the mind and spirit."[13]

Nor can this introduction follow the story of Neill as the chaplain of Minnesota's famous Civil War regiment, the First Minnesota Volunteer Infantry, save to note that in a sermon delivered to the soldiers before they departed from Fort Snelling for Washington, Neill said, "Your errand is not to overturn, but to uphold the most tolerant and forbearing government on earth." The soldiers were going away to fight "misguided brethren, not with wrathful, but with mourning hearts."[14] His service as chaplain began in June, 1861, and continued until July, 1862. Ostensibly he resigned from his regimental service to accept an appointment as chaplain of the United States Military Hospital of Philadelphia, of which his brother John was the head. Little is known about Neill's work in Philadelphia from 1862 until his resignation as hospital chaplain in January, 1864. In general it may be said, however, that Neill was critical of the services of chaplains in the army. He believed that their selection by regiments was wrong in principle and that the ministers chosen did not fairly represent the better talents of the churches of the country. He wanted to see a national clerical board set up by Congress; a screening of chaplains for competency; and Presidential appointments, not exceeding one hundred, of brigade chaplains to replace those originally chosen by regiments. Neill was not alone in his condemnation of the system. On one occasion three ministers of different denominations called on Lincoln to recommend a change, since, in their judgment, many chaplains were not properly qualified.[15]

In February, 1864, Neill was appointed to a position

[13] Folwell, *History of Minnesota*, 4:434–442; and Buck, in *Dictionary of American Biography*, 13:408.
[14] Dupre, *Neill*, 67.
[15] Drafts of Neill's statements on the selection of chaplains and of a proposed law to reform the system are in the Neill Papers. See also, Sandburg, *War Years*, 3:326.

which in effect was that of assistant secretary to President Lincoln. Though nominally in the Department of the Interior, Neill's assignment was actually to the Executive Mansion. There, working with the President's chief secretary, John G. Nicolay, and with assistant secretary John Hay, he had the duty of going over and arranging the President's daily mail and also of signing land patents. That Neill's name was familiar in the White House as early as 1862 is known, for on July 23 of that year his *History of Minnesota* was drawn out from the Library of Congress in the name of President Lincoln (and it was returned on December 24).[16] A plausible explanation is that the President in July, 1862, had asked Nicolay to go to Minnesota, there to meet William P. Dole, the commissioner of Indian affairs, and to work out a land cession treaty with the Chippewa bands in northwestern Minnesota. Unquestionably Nicolay wanted to post himself on Minnesota backgrounds and problems and therefore consulted Neill's book. That this is more than conjecture is proved by a letter to Neill written by Nicolay on August 4, 1862, at Springfield, Illinois. In it he writes, "I find, on arriving here, your 'History of Minnesota' which you kindly promised to forward. I am glad to have it to take with me on my trip up north. Please accept my sincere thanks for the present."[17] The mission of Nicolay and Dole unhappily collided with the Sioux Uprising, which began on August 18, 1862. The two emissaries attempted to deal with the Chippewa chief, Hole-in-the-Day, but in September the negotiations collapsed. Early in 1863 Nicolay published magazine ar-

[16] In *Abraham Lincoln, A New Portrait*, 1:369–371 (New York, 1931), Emanuel Hertz lists all the books taken out of the Library of Congress by President Lincoln or in his name.

[17] Nicolay's letter is in the Neill Papers. In 1863 Neill presented a copy of the illustrated edition of his *History of Minnesota* to President Lincoln. See his letter to Lincoln, January 28, 1863, and a letter of the same date to Nicolay, in which he expressed the hope that the President would write a personal acknowledgment, in the Abraham Lincoln Papers, Library of Congress. The Minnesota Historical Society has copies of these documents.

EDWARD D. NEILL IN 1861   (*Minnesota Historical Society*)

ticles dealing with Hole-in-the-Day and the Sioux Uprising.[18]

Against this background there is every reason to believe that Helen Nicolay, a daughter of John Nicolay, is correct in her explanation of Neill's appointment. She writes that when William O. Stoddard was incapacitated by illness, her father asked to have Neill appointed to the place. The position was a clerkship in the Department of the Interior, its chief duty the signing of land patents; but Stoddard had been moved to the White House because he could sign the land patents there and also give needed help to Nicolay and Hay in the handling of the mail and in performing sundry errands.[19] It was such a combination of duties that Neill took over, beginning in February, 1864. From that time to the end of Lincoln's life he was in daily touch with the affairs of the White House. He thus had the opportunity of observing and working with the great President during the final fourteen months of the administration.

Certainly it was no ordinary man that Nicolay had selected as a secretarial assistant. Yet, taking into account Neill's education, experience, and capacity as a scholar and writer, it must be confessed that the routine duties assigned to him were very humble. But he had not been long at the White House before he was entrusted with duties more responsible than those of sorting mail and

[18] John G. Nicolay, "Hole-in-the-Day," in *Harper's New Monthly Magazine*, 26:186–191 (January, 1863); and "The Sioux War," in *Continental Monthly*, 3:195–204 (February, 1863). See also Ella Hawkinson, "The Old Crossing Chippewa Treaty and Its Sequel," in *Minnesota History*, 15:285 (September, 1934).

[19] Helen Nicolay, *Lincoln's Secretary: A Biography of John G. Nicolay*, 87, 151–155 (New York, 1949). Roy P. Basler, ed., *The Collected Works of Abraham Lincoln*, 7:514n (New Brunswick, N.J., 1953), writes that Neill on August 23, 1864, was given an appointment as the President's secretary for the signing of patents after having served in a similar capacity "while second class clerk in the Department of the Interior." The official appointment, signed by Lincoln, is in the Neill Collection, Macalester College, as is a reappointment for four years from March 3, 1865, signed by Lincoln on March 9, 1865. On Stoddard, see William O. Stoddard, Jr., ed., *Lincoln's Third Secretary: The Memoirs of William O. Stoddard* (New York, 1955).

signing the President's name to land patents from the Department of the Interior.

John Hay, who many years later became United States ambassador to Britain and American secretary of state, was then — still in his twenties — a member of Lincoln's modest corps of secretaries. There is evidence that he was aware of the competence of Neill. In the Minnesota Historical Society's Neill Papers is an original letter written to Neill by Hay on July 14, 1864, in the absence of Nicolay. Not heretofore published (as far as is known), its text is as follows:

> I am going to New York tonight on business. Will be gone only a very few days.
> I leave matters in your hands till my return. There will probably be little to do. Refer as little to the President as possible. Keep visitors out of the house when you can. Inhospitable, but prudent.
> I have a few franked envelopes. Let matters of ordinary reference go without formality of signature. If you have any doubt about any matter, please reserve it till my return.

How long Neill acted for Hay is not known. There is a gap in the Hay diary and letters from July 14 to August 25. In late August and early September, he was in Illinois. That Neill's duties became, with time, less routine than they were at the outset is evident also from an undated manuscript fragment in the Neill Papers, written after the President's death. In this, Neill explained that during the President's last year, because of the ill health and heavy duties of Nicolay, he had to "act as his Assistant to open and read all letters directed to the President & select therefrom such as I thought needed his attention." Neill also drafted telegrams, letters, and notes which were signed by Lincoln or Nicolay, or both.[20]

[20] Tyler Dennett, *Lincoln and the Civil War in the Diaries and Letters of John Hay*, 210–215 (New York, 1939). For the papers drafted by Neill and in his handwriting, see Basler, *Collected Works*, 7:252n, 514n, 529n; 8:136n, 273, 299n. A curious item is an endorsement on a petition from New York (March 4, 1862) recommending James L. Pettigru for ap-

INTRODUCTION 13

In the first of the documents here printed, Neill looks at the human qualities of Lincoln and illustrates them with episodes that stand out in his memory.[21] The portrait he presents fits in with the interpretation of Abraham Lincoln as a very great man, but the account has the freshness of firsthand impressions. Neill was by nature inclined to be a little pompous, but in his descriptions he seems to have absorbed something of Lincoln's own simplicity. Thus he noted that the President never used "great, swelling words."

Lincoln's patience, his self-control, his firmness in standing by decisions once they had been thought out, and his cheerful readiness to accept responsibility — these traits Neill puts into his word portrait. He also pays tribute to Lincoln's unusual capacity for work. The hot and sultry days of summer in Washington did not slow him down, and he was able to concentrate in the midst of appalling distractions. His accessibility to the public is of course well known, but Neill illustrates it vividly. "No one," he writes, "was too poor to be received," and he says that Lincoln called his daily receptions "the Beggars' Opera." He does not cite the familiar story, recorded by the artist Francis B. Carpenter, that the receptions were "public-opinion baths" which the President found "renovating and invigorating" to his "perceptions of responsibility and duty."[22] Inevitably the recollections tell also of Lincoln's magnanimity and humor.

For many readers the section of the *Reminiscences* devoted to "Curious Correspondence" and the article on "President Lincoln's Mail Bag" will have special interest. Neill takes his readers behind the scenes to see the kind

pointment to the Supreme Court. The endorsement, dated February 16, 1865, reads: "Mr. Neill may have this. A. Lincoln." Basler, *Collected Works,* 8:302.

[21] The main outlines of Neill's appraisal of Lincoln had been shaped many years before and were sketched in a letter written by him in Washington the day after Lincoln died, when, as Neill said, the houses of rich and humble alike were draped in black. His letter was printed in the *St. Paul Daily Press,* April 27, 1865.

[22] Carpenter, *The Inner Life of Abraham Lincoln: Six Months at the White House,* 281 (New York, 1868).

of mail that poured in upon the President. The letters were many indeed, and not a few of them were very long. The nature of Lincoln's mail became well understood by the public when the central collection was opened by the Library of Congress in 1947. The story of that collection is told in detail by Mr. David C. Mearns in his two-volume work *The Lincoln Papers,* but the selections he presents go only to July 4, 1861, whereas Neill necessarily bases his story upon correspondence toward the end of Lincoln's presidency. He draws his illustrations in part from memory, in part from letters that he was permitted to retain after Lincoln's death.[23]

Most, but not all, of the letters to Lincoln in the Neill Papers are from 1864 and 1865. For instance, an admirer in 1862 enclosed with a letter a half dozen "likenesses" of the President woven in silk. A veritable dissertation on the "Rebellion of the Southern States" by a language teacher in Philadelphia, Philippe Gutbub, bears a notation that he wrote it in 1862, but he did not mail it until early in 1865. A woman sent the President her photograph with a letter beginning thus: "Pres Lincon god bless you." Someone in Scotland wrote a lengthy letter signed "Veritas." War or no war, a Catholic bishop in Richmond, Virginia, felt it his duty to make a visit once every ten years to Rome, and, not wishing to face the hazards of the blockade, he asked for a safe conduct to New York by way of Baltimore. He explained that the secretary of war, Edwin M. Stanton, had already refused

[23] Mearns, *The Lincoln Papers: The Story of the Collection With Selections to July 4, 1861* (Garden City, N.Y., 1948). Neill was deeply interested in Lincoln records, and his papers include a number of letters from Lincoln's son Robert, all related to Neill's efforts to obtain such materials. One of them, dated November 20, 1868, gave Neill permission to place in the archives of the Minnesota Historical Society the manuscript of Lincoln's message to the Senate of December 11, 1862, with reference to the "Indian barbarities." Neill also secured for the Society the original of the President's letter of December 6, 1862, to Brigadier General Henry H. Sibley, ordering the hanging of thirty-nine Sioux for crimes committed during the uprising of 1862. See the Minnesota Historical Society's *Annual Report* for 1868 and "Lincoln's Sioux War Order," in *Minnesota History,* 33:77–79 (Summer, 1952).

him permission to go through the lines, and he therefore turned to Stanton's chief. One writer strongly urged the President to announce a plan under which all slaves would be set free through governmental purchase and that a scheme of colonization should be worked out. A humble Kentuckian wrote, "I am a right loyal frend of yours and hails from old kaintuck your humbl wel wisher Isral putnam Winchester."

A "faithful high way preacher and peace maker" informed "Abraham Lincoln and Lady" (January 31, 1865) that he would appear that day in front of the Executive Mansion "with my cart which I draw through the country." Many letters beg the President to commute the sentences of men who were to be hanged, in one case even a Rebel spy. A writer interceded for the "editor of a one horse concern of a Democratic Paper." This editor was "more fool than knave," but he had been found guilty of discouraging enlistments. A high officer praised Lincoln and enclosed a picture of himself for the President. Someone submitted a hymn for the country. There were special letters of introduction, including one from Montgomery Blair, postmaster general in the President's cabinet, introducing a grandnephew of Henry Clay.

In a long, vile letter in the Neill Papers, written in rhyme, an anonymous correspondent threatens President Lincoln's life, calls on him to bend his "Stubborn Knee," and adds:

> This is the Last Warning Unto Thee
> Lincoln!!! That ever you will have from me.

The writer tells the President that his blood will be on his own head "throughout all Eternity." Neill says nothing about such threats in his mailbag article, but in his *Reminiscences* he tells of a sinister warning that he believed was written by someone who knew of the murderous designs of John Wilkes Booth. And in the Neill Papers is a letter from Alexander Ramsey (November 6, 1864), in which he forwards from Minnesota a rumor he has heard that the President, if re-elected, would be assassinated by "the knights."

Lincoln himself, after an oral warning from his friend and personal guard, Ward Hill Lamon, asked, "What does anybody want to assassinate me for? If anyone wants to do so, he can do it by day or night, if he is ready to give his life for mine. It is nonsense." It was not nonsense — there was menace in the air; and there is evidence that Lincoln understood. At one time he had filed away eighty threats in an envelope on which he wrote the label "Assassination." When he stuffed the eighty-first into the file, he said to an artist who was then painting his portrait, "I know I am in danger; but I am not going to worry over threats like these." [24]

After the assassination, Neill served under President Johnson to the end of his term of office in 1869, except for an interlude in 1867 and 1868 when he was a secretary under the eminent schoolman Henry Barnard in the short-lived federal department of education.[25] Neill's duties during the Lincoln year had kept him busy, but he never abandoned his historical interests. The Library of Congress was near at hand, and he found time to explore some of its documents for colonial history, a field that fascinated him. Through the kindness of a neighbor in Beltsville, a village outside Washington where he lived, he was given access to various letters and reports written to Lord Fairfax by George Washington when he was a surveyor. Neill took great interest in these precious records, published some of them, and was given a few which now are preserved in the library of Macalester College, in St. Paul. It was during the years after Lin-

[24] On Lincoln's attitude, see Sandburg, *War Years*, 4:240–246.
[25] Neill resigned from his White House assignment on April 25, 1867. He took much interest in the abortive department of education and as chief clerk wrote at least two published reports. When the department was abolished in 1868, he returned to the White House at the request of President Johnson to handle, among other duties, the revision of Presidential messages. Johnson to Neill, April 25, 1867; William G. Moore to Neill, February 26, 1868, Neill Papers.

coln's death, however, and while Neill was working under President Johnson, that his historical studies blossomed in book after book. His production included *Terra Mariae* (Philadelphia, 1867); *The Fairfaxes of England and America* (Albany, 1868); *Pocahontas and Her Companions* (Albany, 1869); and *History of the Virginia Company of London* (Albany, 1869).[26]

That Neill had a period of anxious concern in his work under President Johnson is evident from an undated manuscript of his in the Neill Papers. Seemingly it was the unfinished draft of a letter or statement acknowledging the receipt of a current report of the Board of Education in St. Paul, sent to him presumably by some friend whose name does not appear. The manuscript, as is proved by internal evidence, was written while President Johnson was in Chicago on his unfortunate "swing around the circle" — that is, early in September, 1866.

The suspension of business, during the President's absence, recalled to Neill the "awful silence when the murdered Lincoln lay in one of the chambers awaiting the funeral ceremonies." In a somber mood Neill considered whether, in "adhering to the present administration," he was in fact "supporting the policy of Mr Lincoln." He quoted, from familiar sources in letters and speeches, some of Lincoln's basic views, and he commented on the strength of the early opposition to those views, especially in Congress. Opposition diminished after the election of 1864, but Neill believed that there was "always a large class" who regarded Lincoln as overly generous to those in insurrection to the government.

Neill noted that when Johnson took over the Presiden-

[26] In his *Terra Mariae,* Neill uses the subtitle *Threads of Maryland Colonial History,* and on the title page he lists himself as "One of the Secretaries of the President of the United States." In his preface, dated February 1, 1867, at "Anacostan Ridge," near Washington, he writes, "When not employed in official duties at the Executive Mansion, it has been a recreation to visit the Capitol, and pushing by the jostling throng, constantly shuffling over the marble tiles of the rotunda, to hasten into the quiet alcoves of the library of Congress." While rummaging in the library he "picked out a few threads" of Maryland's history.

tial office on April 15, 1865, he was fresh from scenes of border warfare and shocked by an act "which veiled the whole nation in crepe." In this setting he made heated statements about punishing traitors. He was "perfectly sincere" in these statements, Neill thought, but the "longer he sat in Mr Lincoln's chair the more he was convinced that a conciliatory policy was the only one for a public statesman to pursue."

His secretary came to the conclusion that Johnson was following in Lincoln's footsteps. The course taken by the government during and since the war, Neill asserted, was "worthy of a great nation." To this he made a single exception: the "manacling of a feeble prisoner like Jefferson Davis." This, to Neill, was an "act of pusil lanimity." He added that he did not know who had instigated it. The incomplete draft ends with a few comments on Negro suffrage. Neill expressed grave doubts about according the right to vote to persons who could not read or write or who lacked "a certain amount of property."

In the light of this statement from 1866, it is of interest to note a letter written to Neill in 1869 by President Johnson's secretary, William G. Moore. Neill had presented his resignation on March 3, and Moore, for the President and himself, expressed esteem for Neill's "accurate information relative to public men and measures" in all periods of American history; for his valuable aid in discharging "the more important duties pertaining to a position in the Executive Office"; for his "devotion to Mr. Lincoln's memory"; and for his "freedom from party and personal prejudices" notwithstanding the fact that he held "decided views." [27]

Other papers from the Civil War period give information about a cause which appealed to Neill's sympathies. On December 19, 1864, he wrote to Lincoln proposing that national recognition should be accorded the "volunteer matrons" who had given service in the United States

[27] Moore to Neill, April 9, 1869, Neill Papers.

general hospitals. He had learned that "not a few devout women" from the beginning of the war had devoted "their whole time, and cultivated energies, as well as a portion of their means, to the amelioration of the condition of the sick and wounded inmates." They had no thought of reward, and their help had been valuable to the surgeons in preserving the "morale" of the hospitals.

As a specific recommendation, Neill suggested that the President, through the surgeon general, should issue "an appropriate diploma to every lady who has for three years, gratuitously and continuously devoted her time to hospital service." An endorsement on Neill's letter by Nicolay states that it was referred by the President to the surgeon general "for report as to the propriety of taking the action proposed by memorialist." A further endorsement by the surgeon general, Joseph K. Barnes, reported that a draft of an "honorary Diploma or certificate of merit" would be submitted for "the approbation" of the President. Neill's idea was adopted, and he evidently was called upon to aid in the writing of the certificate. A voluntary hospital worker in Philadelphia wrote Neill on January 2, 1865, complimenting him on what must have been a draft — a memorial, she said, that "will give pleasure to many a faithful woman." On June 30, 1865, she wrote him again to express her own gratitude for having received a certificate from the surgeon general.[28]

After withdrawing from his secretarial post in Washington, Neill accepted appointment as the United States consul at Dublin, Ireland, an office that he held from 1869 to 1871. With his official duties in Dublin he managed to combine the study of numerous historical documents in Ireland and England; and it was during his Irish stay that he published a substantial book on *The English Colonization of America during the Seventeenth Century* (London, 1871). He had gone carefully into contem-

[28] Neill's letter is in the Abraham Lincoln Collection of the Library of Congress; the Minnesota Historical Society has a copy. Hannah M. Davis to Neill, January 2 and June 30, 1865, Neill Papers.

porary sources, and he was aware that his findings contradicted statements by various eminent writers. "Myths creep into history," he wrote in his preface, "as noiselessly as book-worms between the leaves of an old volume, and it is as difficult to dislodge the former, as the latter."

Neill's activities as consul have not yet been described in detail on the basis of his own correspondence and the consular archives. As a scholar Neill unquestionably appreciated the richness of historical materials available in England and Ireland, and his correspondence shows that he visited many libraries and other institutions and also met some notable men. He had been away from Minnesota for a decade, however, and he wanted to go home. Though separated from the state physically, he had kept in close touch with Minnesota friends and institutions; and when he resigned from the consulate in December, 1871, he returned to his own state not as a stranger but as a Minnesotan ready to resume and carry forward his inveterate interests in education, scholarship, and the church.

After his return to St. Paul, historical writing commanded much of his energy, but more and more during the last two decades of his life, his fortunes were linked with the emerging Macalester College. This institution was his brain child, his major dream. He was the founder and inspirer of the college. While it was being planned and organized but before it actually became a functioning college in 1885, he was officially its president. In his later years, until his death in 1893 at the age of seventy, he was Macalester's professor of history, literature, and political economy. This was an appropriate recognition of the breadth of his interests and the priority of history among the enthusiasms that dominated his life.

Neill could on occasion be individualistic, irascible, and unpredictable, and his firm opposition to coeducation brought about unhappy relationships with his college colleagues in his later years. At one time the trustees censured him, but he brushed their censure aside with the remark that he was not an appointee of the trustees. Because of coeducation he sulked, and shortly before his death he blithely informed the trustees that he would resume his classes whenever he was given assurance that they would consist only of young men. If he seemed out of step with some educational trends, he was ahead of his times in other respects. In 1891 he proposed a "roving professorship of American institutions" for a wide public, with some half dozen colleges and universities sponsoring lectures. He advocated similar professorships in several other fields, but nobody followed his lead; and so in 1891 and 1892 he gave his idea a trial run by delivering a half dozen lectures on American government in each of three Minnesota cities.[29]

His passion for writing and publishing continued to the end of his career and in fact reached a very high creative point during the very last years. He had made a major contribution to the fourth volume of Justin Winsor's *Narrative and Critical History of America,* published in 1884,[30] but in some respects his most amazing scholarly achievement was a series of *Macalester College Contributions* issued between 1890 and 1892 by that college's department of history, literature, and political science. The department was Neill himself.

The *Contributions,* in three series, comprised in all twenty-five historical essays, every one of them written by Neill. Twelve essays appeared in the first series, an equal number in the second, and there cannot be the slightest doubt that he intended to write a round dozen articles for the third series. Unhappily he succeeded in finishing only one piece for that group. It is not, of course, their number that makes them noteworthy, though the magnitude of what he did is impressive enough. The articles drew much upon Neill's researches of the preceding

[29] Dupre, *Neill,* 97–110.
[30] Neill has an elaborately documented chapter in Winsor's fourth volume, pages 163–200 (Boston and New York). The subject is "Discovery along the Great Lakes."

years, but the twenty-five pieces were not reprints. Fresh in scholarship and writing, intrinsically interesting, they indicate the sweep of history that appealed to his imagination. There were biographical studies of Christopher Columbus, John Smith, Benjamin Franklin, Francis Bacon, Paul Marin (a French fur trader of the eighteenth century), and William T. Boutwell, missionary to the Indians. He also wrote about the medical history of the American Revolution, early fur-trading activities on Lake Superior, the sources of the Mississippi River, the story of the St. Croix Valley, and various other topics. The articles are a monument to his creative zeal as he neared the age of three score years and ten.[31]

Macalester College also benefited from Neill's zeal for collecting both manuscripts and books. As early as 1882 he promised to give five hundred books from his private collection for the college library.[32] This promise was more than redeemed, for today the Neill collection contains some fifteen hundred to two thousand volumes or more. It is the quality rather than the size of the collection that gives it lasting importance, however. Neill's books include not a few rarities, first editions, basic works of value and interest. Like the Neill Papers preserved by the Minnesota Historical Society, the Neill books at Macalester College are a permanent monument to the restless, ambitious, versatile, and productive man thus honored. Because of what Neill was, believed in, and did, he exerts an ongoing influence. This centers in education and scholarship, but it is also associated with patriotic service at a critical time in the nation's history.

[31] Commenting on the first series of *Contributions,* Frederick Jackson Turner wrote Neill that they were "of interest and service not only to the people of the Upper Mississippi valley, but of the entire Northwest as well." Turner to Neill, August 26, 1890, Neill Papers. In another (and undated) letter, Turner spoke of Neill's "most valuable service" in his work on the French fur traders. The Neill Papers contain letters from many other historians, including Justin Winsor, Reuben Gold Thwaites, and Elliott Coues.

[32] Neill also offered original autographs of William Penn and George Washington. Dupre, *Neill,* 87.

INTRODUCTION 23

Relatively few footnotes have been appended to the *Reminiscences* and the account of the mailbag, since many of the events touched upon are familiar and can be checked in Lincoln biographies and the various editions of his speeches, messages, and letters. The topical divisions as given in the original printed version of the *Reminiscences* have been retained. The text of the mailbag essay is taken from the original manuscript without change save that in an instance or two the editor has added periods at the ends of sentences where they seem to have been omitted in the original. Neill was a writer of much experience who would not have let a paper go into print without finishing its punctuation.

Reminiscences of the Last Year of President Lincoln's Life

ONE of the most intelligent and extensive manufacturers of Dublin, whose father at the time was a representative of that city in the British Parliament, after the transaction of some business in the American consulate, said to me, "Now tell me something about President Lincoln." [1]

The remark was not singular, but expressed the desire which after the war prevailed in all the countries of Europe to know more of him who has left a name which the world will not willingly let die.

The paper which has been prepared is not an elaborate essay, nor will it betray any confidence, nor will it cherish partisanship, but will only give a few reminiscences of President Lincoln, who, in virtue of his office, was commander-in-chief of that army and navy, many of whose officers are now members of the Loyal Legion of the United States.

On the 21st of June, 1861, the First Minnesota Infantry Regiment, amid the cheers and tears of hundreds, embarked in steamboats from Jackson Street, in the city of St. Paul, for the valley of the Potomac River.[2] The next week the regiment was encamped on vacant squares east of the Capitol in Washington, and one day, in the morn-

[1] This is, of course, a reminiscence from the time when Neill served as the United States consul at Dublin, 1869–71.

[2] A comprehensive and critical history of the regiment is given by John Q. Imholte in *The First Volunteers; History of the First Minnesota Volunteer Regiment, 1861–1865* (Minneapolis, 1963).

ing papers, it was announced that in the afternoon the President would assist in raising a flag on the grounds south of his residence; and never having seen Mr. Lincoln, I went there with some other officers of the regiment. The crowd was very great. On the balcony of the President's house sat General [Winfield] Scott, in full uniform, looking as majestic as old Jupiter of the ancient sculptors, while on a temporary platform around the flag-staff stood the President, ready to pull at a given signal. Among the spectators directly before me stood a man, plainly dressed, with serious countenance, with his wife by his side, who was then known as Governor Andrew Johnson, of Tennessee. Several years after, Mr. Johnson, referring to this occasion, said an occurrence took place which the superstitious would have considered an ill omen. He told me the President pulled the rope too long, so that the bunting of the flag was split, and he could but think at the time that he might be pained by the calamity of the great republic rent in twain permanently.

President Lincoln was not again seen by me until after the First Minnesota Regiment had the fiery trials at Bull Run, Fair Oaks, and the Seven Days' battles terminating on Malvern Hill. Early in July, 1862, while the Army of the Potomac was resting around Harrison's Landing, on the James River, impelled by patriotism, and impressed by the gravity of the situation, he came down to look General [George B.] McClellan in the face, and aid him to the extent of his power.[3]

Attracted by cheering, I looked in the direction from which it came, and saw two horsemen. One had short legs, but a fine body and presence above the hips, and was on a large horse, in military dress. It was General McClellan. The other, six feet four inches in height, upon a smaller horse, so that his feet seemed very near the ground, dressed as a civilian, with a tall silk hat, was Abraham Lincoln. As he rode in front of the army the shouts of thousands of weary men showed that his pres-

[3] Lincoln's visit to Harrison's Landing, with Secretary of War Stanton, occurred on July 8, 1862. Sandburg, *War Years*, 1:495.

ence had cheered them; yet no soldier who saw him that day, looking so much like the typical Brother Jonathan of the caricatures, can ever forget the scene.

Early in 1864 I was appointed to read and dispose of all letters addressed to President Lincoln, and commissioned as secretary to sign land patents. A mail-bag was brought to my room at the President's mansion twice a day, well filled with letters upon various subjects.

Every month my impression of the greatness of President Lincoln increased. He was above a life of mere routine. In his bearing there was nothing artificial or mechanical. While he desired to be appreciated, and estimated [*esteemed?*] the honors conferred upon him, he was never puffed up, nor used great, swelling words. In conversation I never knew him to speak of himself as President, but when necessary to allude to his position, he would use circumlocution, and say, "Before I came here," or something equivalent. He was independent of all cliques. Willing to be convinced, with a wonderful patience he listened to the opinions and criticisms of others. Those whose opinions were not accepted would sometimes charge that he was under the thumb of this or that man, but the sequel always proved that he was not a party tool. While he did not frown, nor stamp his feet, while he eschewed the language of the Janus-faced diplomat, and was slow to reach a conclusion, yet when an opinion was deliberately formed he was as firm as a rock. At critical periods he was prompt to assume responsibility.

HIS TRIP TO FORTRESS MONROE

On the morning of the 2d of February, 1865, between nine and ten o'clock, as I was ascending the stairs to the second story, to reach my room, I met [Charles] Forbes, an intelligent servant, descending with a small valise in his hand, and I asked, "Where are you going?" Looking up to see that no one was near, he whispered, "Fortress Monroe," and hurried on. When I reached the upper hall I met the President with his overcoat, and going to my room, looked out of the window, and saw him quietly walking around the curved pavement which leads to Pennsylvania Avenue, while Forbes was following, at a distance of two or three hundred feet, as his valet. Waiting for some time, I then crossed the hall to the room of the principal secretary, Mr. John G. Nicolay, and quietly said, "The President has left the city." "What do you mean?" he asked; and I replied, "Just what I have said." Rising quickly, he opened the door which communicated with the President's room, and was astonished to find the chair of Mr. Lincoln vacant. The President had received a despatch which convinced him that it was proper to go to Fortress Monroe and confer with the rebel commissioners, Alexander Stephens, R. M. T. Hunter, and J. A. Campbell, and at nine o'clock that morning sent the following telegram to Secretary [William H.] Seward, already there: "Induced by a despatch from General Grant, I join you at Fortress Monroe."[4]

The failure of this conference to restore peace has become a part of our history, and upon it it is unnecessary to dwell. Upon the return of the President, Forbes told me that the rebel commissioners seemed to be very friendly, and that after they returned to the steamboat, which was to take them back to the vicinity of Richmond, a negro was sent in a row-boat by Mr. Seward with a basket of champagne, to be presented with his compliments. After the man reached the deck the commissioners read the note, and waved their handkerchiefs in acknowledgment, and then Mr. Seward, speaking through a boatswain's trumpet, said, "Keep the champagne, but return the negro." The status of the negro, in case of cessation of hostilities, had been one of the subjects discussed in the conference.

A GREAT WORKER

The President's capacity for work was wonderful. While other men were taking recreation through the

[4] An account of the Hampton Roads Conference is given in Sandburg, *War Years*, 4:32-43.

sultry months of summer, he remained in his office attending to the wants of the nation. He was never an idler or a lounger. Each hour he was busy. At the election in November, 1864, he was chosen President for a second term. Anxious to know the returns from the several States the morning after the election, I came to the mansion earlier than usual. As I passed the door of his office, which was ajar, I saw that he was at his table and engaged in official work.[5] Entering the room, I took a seat by his side, extended my hand, and congratulated him upon the vote, for my country's sake and for his own sake. Turning away from the papers which had been occupying his attention, he spoke kindly of his competitor, the calm, prudent general and great organizer, whose remains this week have been placed in the cold grave. He told me that General Scott had recommended McClellan as an officer who had studied the science of war, and had been in the Crimea during the war against Russia, and that he told Scott that he knew nothing about the science of war, and it was very important to have just such a person to organize the raw recruits of the republic around Washington.

In June, 1864, he was persuaded to attend a great fair in Philadelphia, under the auspices of the Sanitary Commission, and returned one morning about ten o'clock.[6] As official business had accumulated during his absence, as soon as he entered the house he went immediately to his office. In less than an hour I went to see him, and found him stretched out, his head on the back of one chair, his legs resting on another, his collar and cravat on the table, a mulatto barber lathering his face, while the Attorney-General, Edward Bates, was quietly seated by his side, talking to him upon some matter of state. It was a striking illustration of his desire to be at work. To the

[5] The election day was November 8, 1864. Lincoln had spent much of the night at the War Department receiving election returns. Benjamin P. Thomas, *Abraham Lincoln*, 452 (New York, 1952).

[6] Lincoln's speech at the fair, delivered June 16, is in Basler, *Collected Works*, 7:394-396. See Sandburg, *War Years*, 3:52.

question whether his visit was pleasant, he replied that it was, and the ladies, he believed, had made several thousand dollars by placing him on exhibition.

His memory was very retentive. During the last year of the war a convalescent soldier at Elmira Hospital, New York, while strolling with a fellow-soldier, administered some drug to him and robbed him. From the effect of the drugging the plundered man died, and the robber was tried by court-martial and sentenced to be hung. His friends obtained a suspension of sentence on the ground that he was insane. The testimony in the case was sent to a physician, the superintendent of a lunatic asylum, and his opinion requested. In due time the doctor's report, covering several foolscap pages, was received by mail, and after being read and endorsed, was sent to the President.

Some weeks after, General James A. Hardie, the assistant adjutant-general at the War Department, came to my room, and said it was very desirable that the President should take some action relative to the soldier whose sentence had been suspended. Going to the President, I told him General Hardie wanted to know about this soldier's papers. Pointing to the top of his desk he merely replied, "There they are; tell him they are still in soak." Hardie, quite chagrined by the unsatisfactory answer, hurried off. In about two weeks he came again and said, "The soldier ought to be hung or pardoned; will you again see the President?" I did as asked, and then the President inquired if I had read the report which came from the doctor. I answered that I had. Then rising, he went to a case filled with papers, and without the slightest difficulty found the report and read its last sentence, which was to this effect: "Although I cannot pronounce the person insane, he certainly is peculiar." "Now," he said, "if these last words had not been written I should have had no hesitation in disposing of this case." Life to him was sacred, and he never would sign a paper that would take away life without deliberation.

As a writer he was fluent and forcible. His papers bore few marks of revision, and while his style was not Ciceronian, it was clear, pure, and easily comprehended. He composed letters amid distractions which would have appalled other men. He kept no formal letter-book. One morning in April, 1864, he came to me with a letter in his hand and said, —

"Perhaps it is well to make a copy. Do so, and send the copy or the original, as you prefer, to the person to whom addressed."

It was his well-known letter to A. G. Hodges, of Frankfort, Kentucky, in which he gave the substance of his conversation with Governor [Thomas E.] Bramlette. The opening sentences were:

"I am naturally anti-slavery. If slavery is not wrong, nothing is wrong. I cannot remember when I did not so think and feel, and yet I have never understood that the Presidency conferred upon me an unrestricted right to act officially upon this judgment and feeling. It was in the oath that I took that I would, to the best of my ability, preserve, protect, and defend the Constitution of the United States. I could not take the office without taking the oath. Nor was it in my view that I might take an oath to get power, and break the oath in using the power."[7]

In February, 1865, he brought me several notes, and said they were the correspondence growing out of the visit of the senior Francis P. Blair to Richmond, and asked if I would arrange and connect them with red tape, so that he could show them to friends. The first was simply a visiting-card, on which, directed to no person, was this brief note:

"Allow the bearer, F. P. Blair, Sr., to pass our lines, go South and return. A. Lincoln."

There was also a letter from Mr. Jefferson Davis to

[7] The letter to Hodges, dated April 4, 1864, is one of the most incisive and famous of Lincoln's letters. The full text has been printed many times. It is in Basler, *Collected Works*, 7:281–283.

Mr. Blair. Mr. Davis in spelling the word negotiation used a "c" in place of the first "t," which is unusual.

PERSONAL TRAITS

President Lincoln's accessibility won the hearts of the people. No one was too poor to be received. When more important business was attended to, on some days, between two and three o'clock in the afternoon, he would have his door thrown open, and all in the hall were allowed to enter and prefer their requests. He playfully called it "the Beggars' Opera."[8]

Mr. [Simon] Cameron, his first Secretary of War, told me he came once while a reception of this kind was being held, and he wondered at the humor, patience, and versatility of Mr. Lincoln.

One woman tried to obtain an order upon the commissary at Washington for provisions for her family on the ground that her husband was a soldier, and was with difficulty convinced that the President could not undertake to feed the families which soldiers had left behind them.

A Gascon in spirit, with imperfect use of the English language, in turn approached the President with a large bundle of papers and the pompous announcement that he spoke six languages, and wished an appointment as consul to some foreign country. With infinite tact he told the persistent man to take the papers to the Secretary of State, and if he would send a commission he would sign it. The sanguine fellow, not dwelling upon the import of that little word "if," left, blessing the President for his goodness and promptness.

At length, Mr. Cameron told me, when comparatively few were left in the room, a young man, who evidently had never been far from the place in which he was born, stood before the President, and was greatly embarrassed. In search of a paper he wished to present he put his hand into his side-pocket, but could not find it; then he began

[8] See Blegen, *Lincoln's Imagery: A Study in Word Power*, 17 (La Crosse, Wis., 1954).

to feel his overcoat-pockets, and became more confused. The President waited patiently, and at last, with a pleasant look, remarked, "Friends, you will remember that some time ago a man stood here who told us he could speak six languages, and now we have one who does not seem able to speak a word." By this time the young man found his paper, and consequently recovered his self-possession. His application was within the power of the President to grant, and the applicant left rejoicing.

Mr. Lincoln's manners were never repulsive. While he could not grace a ball-room, nor compete with the perfumed and spangled representative of a foreign court in a knowledge of the laws of fashion, yet in his heart there was always kindly feeling for others; and thus, in the best sense, he was a gentleman. The late Edward Everett, whose elegance and courtliness of manner no one questioned, met Mr. Lincoln for the first time at the dinner-table of a friend on the occasion of the dedication of the national cemetery at Gettysburg, and he afterwards said that he was impressed with his simple, easy bearing.[9] Destitute of hauteur, and conscious of wishing no man any harm, he had from youth indulged in pleasantry, by telling to farmers at the country store, and to fellow-lawyers while going to court, amusing, if not always classic, stories, not to raise a laugh, but to illustrate his views. This habit remained through life, but no fair-minded man would have called him a trifling jester or a coarse buffoon. It was a relief to him, amid the cares of civil war, to indulge in quaint expressions. One day an elderly gentleman, who wished to give a house as a home for soldiers' orphans, visited him and said "Secretary [Edwin M.] Stanton was not kind, and would not listen to him." A messenger came and said the President wished to see me. When I entered, he wrote on a visiting-card, "Will the Secretary of War please see the gentleman?" and asked me if I would go with the note, and person, to

[9] Everett wrote that Lincoln was the "peer of any person present so far as manners, appearance, and conversation were concerned." Paul R. Frothingham, *Edward Everett, Orator and Statesman*, 453 (Boston, 1925).

REMINISCENCES OF LINCOLN'S LAST YEAR 33

the War Department. General Hardie, when I met him, seemed displeased as he looked at the gentleman, but I told him I had been sent with a note from the President. Hastily taking the card, he went to the Secretary's room, but soon came out, and curtly said, "The Secretary cannot see the gentleman." Persuading the person to go back to the hotel and leave the city until the times were more propitious, I went to the President, showed him the card, and said it had failed to accomplish what was desired. With a look full of humor, he said, "Well! well! the requests of the commander-in-chief don't amount to much."

One morning he told his doorkeeper that he would not be interrupted, as he was much engaged. Senator [Jacob M.] Howard, of Michigan, came and said he must see him. The doorkeeper could not disobey orders, and brought him to me. As soon as he sat down, he showed that he was in ill humor, and said, "If it were his own son he would not act so." Never having seen the Senator, and supposing him to be some agent to procure substitutes, I replied that if he continued to speak disrespectfully of the President, in his own house, I must request him to leave my room. He then said that he was Senator Howard, and that he had come to request suspension of sentence of a soldier who in a few hours was to be executed.

Entering the President's room, I found him very busy in writing, and apologetically said, "Would not have interrupted you, but Senator Howard wants suspension in a certain case." "Wants suspension! Well, that is a queer request." Afterwards he told me to write a telegram, giving the soldier's name, ordering suspension of sentence, sign his name, and send it through the War Department. I told him I would write the order, but preferred that he should sign it.

A drunken black man of a low grade of intellect killed some one with an axe in the suburbs of Washington, and was sentenced to be hung. A question arose as to whether it was the duty of the marshal of the district or some one else to attend to the execution. Early one morning I saw the President in Secretary Nicolay's room, and, as he was not there, I asked if I could do anything. He replied, "There is a dispute as to the hanging of a black man, and I have determined to settle the controversy by not having him hung, and I would like to see Marshal [Ward H.] Lamon."

A commutation of sentence to imprisonment for life was prepared, and Marshal Lamon reached the scaffold as the rope was being fastened around the culprit's neck, and it took some time for the city authorities, and a longer time for the dull-headed negro, to comprehend that there was to be no hanging, and that the paper read by the marshal was a commutation by President Lincoln.

HIS MAGNANIMITY

The President cultivated no animosities, and for the public good would sometimes appoint those who criticised his acts. Major John Hay, the unmarried secretary, one day said to me, "What do you think Mr. Lincoln has done?" Then he told me that he had just nominated Salmon P. Chase as the Chief Justice of the Supreme Court. It was an act of magnanimity, as Mr. Chase had been willing to see him defeated, and had aided in the circulation of a pamphlet giving reasons why he should not be nominated a second time for the Presidency. While Mr. Lincoln was dead and yet unburied, in examining his papers, I found a letter from Mr. Simeon Draper, written as early as 1862, in which he mentioned that Chief Justice [Roger B.] Taney had reached so great an age that his days on earth would be few, and that when his death occurred he hoped Mr. Chase would be his successor.

From the first there was accord between Gen. Grant and the president. In the October number of the *Century Magazine* it is mentioned that after the surrender of Vicksburg the president sent for J. Russell Jones, who had been a merchant in Galena, to visit Washington, and after his arrival said: "I have sent for you, Mr. Jones, to know if that man Grant wants to be president." The

ABRAHAM LINCOLN IN 1864 (*National Archives*)

response was: "No, I have just come from Vicksburg, and I know he wants you re-elected." Then said Mr. Lincoln: "You have lifted a great weight from my mind, and done me an immense amount of good, for I tell you, my friend, no man knows how deeply that presidential grub gnaws till he has had it himself." [10]

The President knew that there were those in his Cabinet and in the army willing to take his seat. Letters had been received mentioning that one of General B. F. Butler's staff officers was visiting in the West, and whispering that the general was willing to be President. Mr. Chase was too willing to be his successor. No wonder it was a relief to know that General Grant had no aspirations in that direction.

About two o'clock in the afternoon of the 9th of March, 1864, a messenger told me to look out of the window of my room and I would see General Grant. I went, and saw a plain, round-shouldered man in citizen's dress, with a lad, his eldest son, by his side, walking away from the house, where he had been to pay his first visit to the President. To gratify the public and appease the reporters, the President wrote the few words which he had spoken when he gave the general his commission upon a piece of paper, partly torn, and Grant penned a brief reply.[11]

During the latter part of 1864, Grant sent a telegram to this effect, indicating his pertinacity: "It seems to me that a call should be issued for more men, but in any event I shall continue and do the best with those I have left."

Early in the spring of 1865 the President sent a telegram to General Grant, as follows: "The financial pres-

[10] This paragraph appears in the first printed version of Neill's address—the paper-bound pamphlet of 1885—but was omitted when the essay was republished in *Glimpses of the Nation's Struggle* in 1887. The incident had been recounted by James Harrison Wilson, "Reminiscences of General Grant," in *Century Magazine*, 30:954 (October, 1885).

[11] Grant's first visit to Washington and to Lincoln is described in many books about Lincoln and Grant. An amusing account is in William E. Woodward, *Meet General Grant*, 308 (New York, 1928).

sure is so great, I hope that you will make an early move and close the war."

Full of anxiety, Mr. Lincoln went to the front during the last days of March, and a movement was begun under General [Philip H.] Sheridan. On the 2d of April Richmond was evacuated, and on the 9th General Lee surrendered.

The President did not exult when there was a victory nor manifest depression when circumstances were adverse.

After our arms had been successful guns were fired in honor of the victory in the public square in front of the mansion. Although the concussion would cause the windows to rattle, he never made allusion to the salutes. He felt that war in any aspect was deplorable, and that one victory did not conquer a peace. Nor was he disturbed when there was an appearance of danger.

During the summer of 1864 I lived in the country thirteen miles from the city, near the junction of the Baltimore and Washington turnpike with the railroad. After breakfast, on Tuesday, July 12, I went, as usual, in a railway-car to the city, and before noon my house was surrounded by General Bradley Johnson's insurgent cavalry, who had made an attempt to capture the New York express-train, and robbed the country store near by of its contents. The presence of the enemy stopped all travel by railroad, and Senator [Alexander] Ramsey, of Minnesota, who happened to be in Washington, found no way to the North except by descending the Potomac to its mouth and then ascending Chesapeake Bay to the city of Baltimore. While the cavalry were in the fields around my house the enemy's infantry was marching towards the capital, by what was called the Seventh Street road, and they set fire to the residence of the Hon. Montgomery Blair, who had been Postmaster-General. As I sat in my room at the President's the smoke of the burning mansion was visible, but business was transacted with as much quietness as if the foe were hundreds of miles distant. Mr. [Gustavus V.] Fox, the Assistant Secre-

REMINISCENCES OF LINCOLN'S LAST YEAR 37

tary of the Navy, had, in a private note, informed the President that if there was any necessity to leave the city, he would find a steamer in readiness at the wharf at the foot of Sixth Street.

About one o'clock of the afternoon of each day of the skirmishing the President would enter his carriage and drive to the forts in the suburbs and watch the soldiers repulse the invaders.[12]

CURIOUS CORRESPONDENCE

The letters sent to the president from day to day were of all descriptions,

"From grave to gay, from lively to severe."

A rude wag, the day after his election for a second term, wrote: "Dear Old Abe, — Yesterday I worked hard for you all day, and wore out my boots. Please send a new pair by mail." After the surrender of General Lee, ropes began to arrive by express, with humorous notes, requesting that they might be used in hanging the late President of the insurgent States upon "a sour apple-tree."

A cheery woman from distant Oregon wrote that the health of her husband had failed, and that it would be a great assistance if he were made postmaster. She continued:

"By the name I bear since my marriage you will not know me, but you will when I tell you that I am Deacon ———'s daughter, at whose house you used to stop in going to court, and you may remember that once, after sewing a button on your coat, you laughingly said, 'I

---

[12] Lincoln was at Fort Stevens on the afternoon of July 12, 1864, and witnessed the skirmishing. While he was standing on a parapet, an officer only a few feet from him was killed by an enemy bullet. Sandburg tells of the incident in his *War Years*, 3:140–143. Men were ordered down, but Lincoln stayed erect until, according to an oft-repeated story, a young captain, not recognizing the President, shouted "Get down, you fool!" The captain was Oliver Wendell Holmes, Jr., later the famous jurist. See John Henry Cramer, *Lincoln Under Enemy Fire*, 22 (Baton Rouge, 1948). Catherine Drinker Bowen in her biography of Holmes adds a phrase alleged to have been spoken by Lincoln, "Captain, I am glad you know how to talk to a civilian." *Yankee from Olympus*, 194 (Boston, 1944).

will not forget you when I am President;' and on another occasion, when my father was making preparation for his quite lengthy evening family prayer, you whispered, 'Go up-stairs and bring down a pillow for me, for I am afraid my knees will become sore.' "

While some letters provoked a smile, others stirred the higher emotions. A sister of the rebel general called Stonewall Jackson told her joy at seeing the Union troops around her farm in Virginia, and how gladly she looked upon the flag of the republic, and the blue uniforms of the officers.

A boy not twenty years of age unfolded a tale of sorrow. He wrote that an elder brother had enlisted, and for some reason had left his regiment, and was marked as a deserter. His parents in consequence were humiliated and heart-broken, and he feared that their days on earth would be shortened in consequence of that word affixed to their son's name. He then begged that the government would take him and allow him to serve the full term of his brother's enlistment, on condition that his brother would be absolved.

A letter once came from Canada, every line of which seemed to be the moan of a burdened conscience. The writer told how he had been skulking for months as a deserter, but that within a short time he had been attending church, had repented and determined to lead a new life. From the hour he had changed his course, although friends dissuaded him, he felt impelled to write to the President, and mention that on a certain day, and at a certain hour, he would be seen walking in the grounds around the mansion, clothed in a certain manner. A messenger was told to be on the watch, and at the time specified he came to my room and said, "The man with the specified overcoat is there." He was then brought up to my room. He had the emaciated face of one who had experienced mental suffering, and willing, if necessary, to die for his transgression. While he waited his letter was sent and explained to the President, who wrote on the back to this effect: "Let this man be returned to his regiment without penalty, except that he shall serve, after the expiration of his term of enlistment, the number of days he was absent by desertion."

Time fails me to relate all that I could, and I will now confine myself to incidents in connection with the last days of the earthly career of this remarkable man.

On Monday, the 9th of April, 1865, the citizens of Washington were full of joy at the intelligence of the surrender of General Lee, and began to throng around the Presidential mansion. On Tuesday morning a procession, with a band of music, arrived while I was conversing with the President, who told the messenger to tell them that he would address them that evening. On that night he delivered his last public address, "not in sorrow, but in gladness of heart," as the opening sentence indicated.[13] At this time Chief Justice Chase was holding court in Baltimore, and on Thursday a letter from him passed through my hands, objecting to some of the phraseology of the President in the address relative to the emancipation proclamation.

It was now evident that, while the war was ended, the work of building up confidence in the government in the late slave States would be herculean, requiring the "wisdom of a serpent and the gentleness of a dove."

On Thursday, I think, he mentioned that he wished to see Mr. John W. Forney, the secretary of the Senate, and also editor of the Philadelphia *Press* and the Washington *Chronicle*. Mr. Forney afterwards told me that he had conferred with him, and suggested that he should make an informal visit to Richmond and other cities of the South, and urge upon editors and leading men the desirableness of their giving a full support to the measures of government. By this method he hoped that enough at least would be persuaded to rally around the flag, so as to obviate the necessity of appointing as postmasters, collectors of revenue, and judges of courts those not natives of the South, with no permanent interest in its wel-

[13] The full text of the final address is in Basler, *Collected Works*, 8:399–405.

fare, who would leave as soon as the emoluments of office ceased. By this time those persons always ready to give advice began to call, and tell what they thought should be done with Mr. Jefferson Davis. Wearied and annoyed, he said to [William H.] Slade, his mulatto doorkeeper, —

"This talk about Mr. Davis tires me. I hope he will mount a fleet horse, reach the shores of the Gulf of Mexico, and drive so far into its waters that we shall never see him again."

The last interview I had with him was between three and four o'clock of the last afternoon of his earthly life. A colonel of a Vermont regiment, who had been on a furlough during his absence from the Army of the Potomac, had been made a brigadier-general. Upon his return he stopped at the War Department for his commission, and was told that it had been sent over to the President for his signature. Coming to the President's house, he told the doorkeeper of the office the occasion of his visit, and he was brought to me. That afternoon there had been a Cabinet meeting and an interview with General Grant, and I went to see the President, and found that he had retired to the private part of the house for a lunch. While I was looking over the papers on his table to see if I could find the desired commission, he came back, eating an apple. I told him for what I was looking, and as I talked he placed his hand on the bell-pull, when I said, "For whom are you going to ring?" Placing his hand upon my coat, he spoke but two words, — "Andrew Johnson." Then I said, "I will come in again." As I was leaving the room the Vice-President had been ushered, and the President advanced and took him by the hand.

None but God knew then that an assassin was preparing plans by which the President in a few hours would be mortally wounded.

After ten o'clock on Friday morning Mrs. Lincoln sent a servant to my room to know whether any complimentary tickets had been received by me, inviting the President and family to attend that night the play of "Our American Cousin" at Ford's Theatre. I replied, "No,"

REMINISCENCES OF LINCOLN'S LAST YEAR 41

and in less than an hour from that time a messenger was sent to the theatre to say that the President's family wished a box. It was not until after that hour that the assassin began to form his plans for that night.

Just at dawn on Saturday morning I was aroused from sleep by a loud pounding, and, going down to the door of my country-house and opening it, found the sergeant of the guard at the railroad crossing, who told me that the President and his Cabinet had been shot, that all travel on the road from Washington had been stopped, and then he burst into tears.

A PREVIOUS WARNING

To me the surprise was not as great as it was to this loyal, tender-hearted soldier. Threatening letters had come to the President through the mails, which did not, however, except in one instance, seem worthy of notice or preservation. That letter was postmarked Gloversville, New York, about forty miles northwest of Albany, during the latter part of February. The handwriting was not at all disguised, but clear and bold. The sentences were brief and those of a person terribly in earnest, and to this effect: "God knows I have hated you, but God knows I cannot be a murderer. Beware of the ides of March. Do not, like Julius Cæsar, go to the Senate unarmed. If I did not love my life, I would sign my name."

The words made such an impression that I consulted with Major John Hay, the unmarried secretary, who slept at the mansion, and whose chamber adjoined my room. He remarked, "What can we do to prevent assassination? The President is so accessible that any villain can feign business, and, while talking to him, draw a razor and cut his throat, and some minutes might elapse after the murderer's escape before we could discover what had been done."

This letter I did not destroy, but some weeks after [David E.] Harold [*Herold*], [Lewis T. P.] Payne, and others had been executed, I gave it to Judge-Advocate-General [Joseph] Holt, who subsequently told me that he had no doubt that the writer had some knowledge of Booth's desire to do evil. Who the writer was will probably never be known.

As no cars were allowed to run, upon the tender of a locomotive I rode to Washington, and reached the house about an hour after the President's body had arrived. A vast crowd was in the streets, a guard of soldiers at each gate, the halls of the mansion, ordinarily filled with visitors, were still, and everything seemed to weep. My position was lonely. Mr. John G. Nicolay, the principal secretary, was absent on a short sea-voyage; Major Hay, by the long watching through the night, was worn out, and lay upon the sofa in his chamber, so that the duty devolved upon me to read and dispose of all the papers that had accumulated in the office since Mr. Lincoln had been President, and make such disposition of them as my judgment suggested. Few men's papers can be found in this world so free from anything objectionable, or sentiments which it would be desirable that the public should not know, as were these.

In the mail received after the President was lying cold with death, there were two which made some impression. One was from General [Ambrose E.] Burnside, resigning his position, thanking the President for the consideration he had always shown, and expressing his willingness, should the nation's life be again endangered, once more to buckle on his sword. The other was written by Chief Justice Chase, at Barnum's Hotel, Baltimore, on Friday night, not long before the fatal shot was fired. Mr. Chase had written on Wednesday relative to the emancipation proclamation, but this second letter was on the position the government should assume toward the late slave population, and in it was asked, "Cannot you take the position of universal suffrage?"

Mr. Lincoln preferred intelligent, impartial suffrage, without respect to color, but was willing to give the right to vote to all colored men who had been soldiers of the United States, even if they could not read.

On Saturday, Slade, the messenger, came to me and said he was very unhappy, and asked me if I had noticed as I crossed the hall to the President's room on Friday afternoon that he was listening to the Vice-President, and nodding assent as he conversed. I told him I had observed him. He then said, —

"It is what I said to Mr. Johnson that makes me feel miserable." The Vice-President had expressed his respect for Mr. Lincoln, but said he thought if he were President he would not make it too easy for the rebels, and that having African blood in his veins he had nodded assent, and expressed the wish that at some future day he might be President.

Assuring him that there was no occasion for his unhappiness, he seemed to be in a measure relieved. Slade was a faithful man, prudent and dignified. He was an elder in the Presbyterian Church for colored people on Fifteenth Street, near the President's mansion.

After the funeral he came to me in a different frame of mind, and told me the ambition of his life was satisfied, that President Johnson had sent for him and made him the steward of the house, which gave him a good salary and some perquisites. He died before Mr. Johnson's term expired, and camellia japonicas were sent by the President to be placed on his coffin, and the President's daughters attended the burial services.

About ten o'clock on Saturday night Major Hay, who had recovered, came to me and said that he thought some one ought to suggest to acting President Johnson that it would be well for him to inform the widow that there was no need of undue haste in leaving the mansion. Going to the National Hotel, I found Senator Ramsey, of Minnesota, in his private parlor, and asked him if he would see Mr. Johnson, to which request he consented. On Sunday morning, about eleven o'clock, the cards of Senators Ramsey and [Daniel S.] Norton were brought to me, and a messenger was sent to Robert, the elder son of the dead President, who came and stood by the table where his father had so lately transacted business. After introducing the Senators, Senator Ramsey delivered the request of President Johnson, that his mother should not feel constrained to leave the house until she had made all proper arrangements.

This son had but a few months before graduated at Harvard University, and his manly bearing on that trying occasion made me feel that he was a worthy son of a worthy father. It is worthy of note that, in after years, he succeeded Senator Ramsey as Secretary of War.

Just before the funeral, President Lincoln's first Secretary of War, Simon Cameron, so long identified with the politics of Pennsylvania, and still living, told me that during his long public career he had never met one who was more sagacious and far-seeing.

Not long after the surrender of Richmond, a native of the South, now a professor in South Carolina, visited me and passed a night. In the chamber where he slept there were on the table some of the advance sheets of [Henry J.] Raymond's "Life of Lincoln," which he had taken up and read. After taking his seat at the breakfast-table, he said that he now believed the caricatures and exaggerations of the peculiarities of the President would soon be forgotten, and that his name would be honored like that of Washington.

The surgeon on duty with the ship "Congress," in the terrible fight with the rebel ram "Merrimac," in Hampton Roads, upon his return from a cruise in the Mediterranean, after the war, told me that he was not only surprised, but gratified, to find in several restaurants in Italy the likeness of Abraham Lincoln.

The words of Paterculus, the historian of the time of one of the Cæsars, relative to a distinguished man of his century, can be aptly applied to him of whom we have spoken: "His distinctive characteristic was this, that he was preceded by none whom he imitated, nor did any come after who could imitate him."

A poet, before Mr. Lincoln's death, well portrayed his future reputation in the following lines:

"No adulation shall the poet bring,
   No o'erwrought picture of thy excellence;
But taught by truthfulness shall simply sing
   The passing worth of cheerful common sense;
Shall call thy honesty a priceless gem,
   Thy patience beautiful, thy faith sublime.
Thy gentle nature let the harsh condemn,
   Just Heaven's reward is in the hand of Time.
Work on amidst the nation's wild turmoil,
   The day of triumph brightens up the sky,
The tree of peace springs up from roots of toil,
   Its leaves shall sweetly crown thee by and by.
Smile on amid thy cares, O Freedom's friend,
   The people's heart is with thee to the end."

President Lincoln's Mail Bag

THE MAIL-BAG of President Lincoln, brought daily by a messenger, from the Post Office to the Executive Mansion was always well filled, especially during the last year of his life.[1] Its contents were different from those that had been hitherto received as communications to Presidents of the United States. The Country was engaged in a momentous struggle for existence; a heart rending civil war was being waged of such magnitude as to elicit the attention of all the nations of earth. Every patriot became intensely interested in the strife, and many after unburdening themselves in prayer before the Unseen, felt that they must sit down and give their thoughts on public affairs to the official head of the Republic.

Then the organization of the man was calculated to draw forth communications from the trustful and sincere. He was what we term a natural man. The prominent traits of his character had not been curbed nor repressed by scholastic discipline, nor had he ever studied the art of etiquette. In the Presidential chair he appeared to his neighbors essentially the same Abraham Lincoln that they had known when they volunteered together, as soldiers to check the movements of the Indian Chief, Black Hawk, or as he sat on the porch of the County Inn telling stories on the evenings of Court Week.

The soubriquet of 'honest old Abe' was bestowed no

[1] In the original manuscript, Neill first used the title "Peeps into President Lincoln's Mail Bag," but he crossed this out.

one exactly knew when, but it became as valid as a baptismal name, and inseparable from the man as the tunic of Nessus.

In the tour from his Illinois home at Springfield to the National Capital previous to his inauguration as President, he passed through many cities and towns and as eager crowds gazed upon his tall spare form, sad but kindly eyes, by no means handsome face, and observed his want of manner, although there was at first a feeling of disappointment, because he did not "look every inch" a President, yet that very absence of official dignity, led to a personal interest, and by the time he was domiciled at the Executive Mansion, loyal men of all parties began to think that he was something more than a sectional President, that he was a patriot who had the welfare of his Country close to his heart, and that he would rule "with malice toward none, with charity toward all."

The fact that he never with "official awe" glanced at any one, and frequently relieved embarrassment by a little story, caused thousands of the sanguine and unsophisticated to take the liberty to write to him not only on the conduct of the war, but to unfold their tale of woe and personal misfortune. To have read all the letters directed to him would have been a Sisyphean labor, never completed, and it was necessarily delegated to another person.[2]

Good and true men without foresight would mail twenty or thirty pages of anxious thought as to the course which they would pursue if in his place, and timid ones would forward manuscripts equally voluminous on the subject of peace at all hazards.

School girls would mail their pretty photographs and in the sauciest little notes ask for his *pretty* face in exchange. College students afflicted with the autograph mania, stormed him with requests for his signature.

[2] The President could read only a small portion of the letters addressed to him. John Hay said that he "did not read one in fifty," and Helen Nicolay, on the basis of notes left by her father, said that Lincoln read "one in a hundred." Mearns, *Lincoln Papers*, 1:38.

An applicant for entrance as a student to the Military Academy at West Point forwarded an accurate description of himself, and stated that he did not possess a form like Apollo, and moreover was *very nearsighted* but added that in reading Plutarch's Lives he had learned that some of the ancient heroes were deformed; he further stated that he was a young Christian, and lifted up with the pride of a novice he strongly urged his appointment, on the ground that the army was much in need of officers of good moral character.

After the day of his election to a second term of office, a wag in New York City wrote, that he had walked his boots out, in securing votes on the previous day, and desired a new pair to be sent by *return mail.* An old Kentuckian sent a large plug of tobacco, as an evidence of his high respect, not knowing that the President though a Kentuckian by birth, eschewed the ancient habit of the Kentucky gentleman, of rolling a "quid" under his tongue, like a sweet morsel.

The lunatics did not forget him, and the pigeon hole of the letter desk labeled "Crazy and Poetry" an odd if not true conjunction, was always filled with contributions. These epistles came not only from Maine and Oregon, but the uttermost parts of the earth, and while many were complimentary, others were imprecatory.

A denunciatory and hortatory religious poem of sixteen foolscap pages came from New Zealand written by a "messenger of the King of Kings and Lord of Lords."

The author stated that he had been absent from England twenty seven years, most of which period was passed in sailing on the coast of New Holland. The insertion of a few lines of the poem will enable each reader to judge whether the inspiration that dictated it was celestial, or derived from the letters of Bull Run [William H.] Russell in the London Times, and copied into all the papers of the distant outposts of the British Realm.[3]

[3] William Russell, the sharp-minded British war correspondent, saw the miserable rout after the first Bull Run and described it vividly.

"At first, the tyrant legions drilled,
   And led by men in war, well skilled,
In numbers, they did far exceed
   Those, Beauregard against them led;
Numbers don't always win the strife,
   Freedom's far more dear than life,
And so it happened on that day,
   The tyrant's legions ran away.
And when the Yankees grew so bold
   Again to boast, it shall be told,
Long as the Sun shall rule the day,
   That at Bull Run, they ran away.

* * *

Like curs they bark, but they cannot bite,
   No courage have they for the fight."

A woman on the distant Pacific coast requested that her husband might be made the postmaster of a small village in Oregon, and in her application stated that the President would remember *her*, as the daughter of a plain and strict Presbyterian, at whose house he used to tarry when a young man, while going or returning from County Courts, and that one night, just before her father commenced his too lengthy evening prayer, he whispered that he wished she would go up and bring him a pillow for his knees, as he feared they might give out, before her parent finished.

A deaf and dumb man who was married had fallen in love with a young girl and supposing that it was in the President's power begged for a divorce promising that if his petition was granted he would go to Church with the new love every Sunday morning.

Some letters were so full of the deepest heart sorrows that the eyes of the reader flooded with tears. A lad eighteen or nineteen years of age states that his parents are heart broken and no longer smile; that his elder brother whom he believed was a brave boy under some

But neither he nor the scornful poet realized that men could "bite"—and win the war — after initial disasters. Thomas, *Abraham Lincoln*, 272.

DATE DUE

AUG 2 4 1999			
GAYLORD			PRINTED IN U.S.A.